The Tara Brooch

Michael Bobb

The Tara Brooch

With images

by

the author

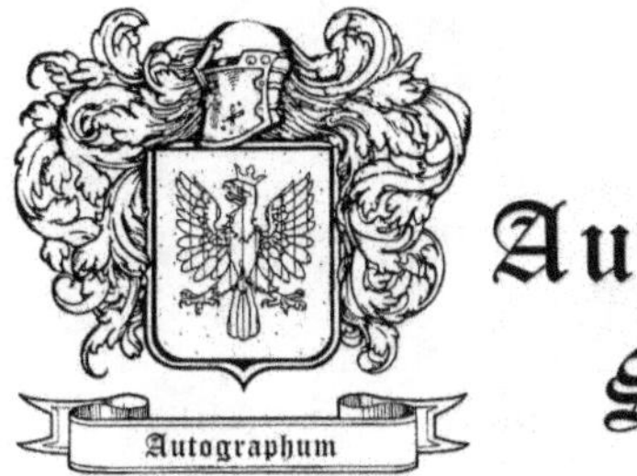

The
Autograph
Score

First published in 2023

by The Autograph Score

www.theautographscore.co.uk

1

Paperback

ISBN 978-1-7392947-2-4

E-book

ISBN 978-1-7392947-3-1

The Autograph Score, London

theautographscore@outlook.com

"So now faith, hope, and love abide,
these three;
but the greatest of these is love"

1 Corinthians 13:13 (ESV)

TABLE OF CONTENTS

LIST OF PLATES

INTRODUCTION

What did he just say?

In this introduction I will be giving you some insights into my poetry. The opening poem in this book is **The Myth Of The Tara Brooch** so let's start there. Now, what would be in my mind when it came to writing this poem? Well, as far as I can remember, I have been drawn to the Celtic way; Celtic ideology, history, music and just about everything Celtic. I happened to be peering inside a volume of an illustrated family encyclopaedia and came across the Tara Brooch. After further research, I set down the poem.

Early one morning I went for a walk in a local park, took a few photographs and put them on social media. One particular comment caught my attention. From this spark, I set about the trilogy: **Good Morning**, **Good Afternoon** and **Good Night**. As I was penning these titles, I found myself writing-in a musical instrument. More on music later.

What are your wildest dreams? What are your, perhaps, more quieter dreams? Can you remember the last dream you had? If you could choose your dreams, what sort of dreams would you choose? In the poem **If Only I Could Dream** I just let my imagination run free: "if only I could dream... if only I could dream..."

In **The Maiden's Dream** I try to get inside the mind of a fair, young woman as she dreams. What sort of things does she dream about? What kind of dream world is she entering into, passing through and coming out of; her thoughts, feelings and surroundings... even longings.

So, as it happened, I was preparing to retire for the evening after drafting a poem. I made a warm drink and was walking around the living room. My eyes looked in the direction of a clock. Almost immediately my mind started composing another poem. I then spent the next couple of hours writing another poem: **Tick-Tock, Tick-Tock.** Apart from the last line, the poem has three lines for each verse and four syllables for each line. In the audiobook recording I have borne this rhythm out.

A few years ago I was in a wood. Lying randomly on the ground just about everywhere I went were bird feathers. I had my camera with me and duly photographed many of them. A few years later I decided to post one of the images on social media with a few rhyming lines. This was the birth of the poem **Feathers** which I extended later and eventually ran into two parts. At the time of writing I had in mind Samuel Taylor Coleridge's Christabel.

Cairns — they fascinate me. Many years ago on my first journey north of the border into Scotland, I came across cairns for the first time. They made an impression on me and I wanted to see them again. Thirty or so years later I went to North Yorkshire and climbed a peak called Ingleborough to see the cairns that were at the top. The experience was truly memorable. And now **The Cairns Of Ingleborough** has been set down. For the audio recording, I married the poem with a song I composed called: Antonia.

Scotland — what can one say? There is so much attractive about the land. The poem **My Everyday Oban** is based on my experience of this part of the world.

These Words Are By Far Few is a love poem. In this case, I point out, gush — romanticism at its "most degenerative". This whole poem is "a byword for sentimentality, frills and rather mindless, if pretty, self-indulgence". And, I agree. Both quotes sourced. It was written where I currently live.

The Armour Of GOD. Starting from the second stanza, the poem looks at the belt of truth. The third looks at the breastplate of righteousness. The fourth looks at the gospel of peace. The fifth looks at the shield of faith. The sixth looks at the helmet of salvation. The seventh looks at prayer.

The Lion Of Judah poem is a stylised literary depiction of Jesus Christ as spoken about in the Bible, particularly the New Testament

— with graphic literary 'imagery' from the last book: Revelation. I use the inverted commas deliberately. And, interestingly, the accompanying music in the audiobook is composed by myself — Greensleeves never sounded so dissonant and ferocious. Hold onto your hats!

N.B. When the Bible was written, there were no chapter headings, no verse numeration and no punctuation.

In **The Ecstasy Of Hildegard** I have combined Saint Hildegard of Bingen with the sculpture of Saint Teresa by Gian Lorenzo Bernini.

I had just left the supermarket. It was a windy day. Passing by a park I saw a kite being flown in the sky. Before I arrived home, I had something of a title in my mind. The finished poem I called: I **Wish I Was A Kite.**

The **Leonardo da Vinci** poem is in limerick form. Four short limericks, four pieces of art — his art. Because they are about art, they are called ekphrastic.

Have you ever thought about extroverted personalities? Have you ever thought about introverted personalities? Have you ever thought about the extrovert/introvert hybrid? The great composer Robert Schumann used the **Florestan And Eusebius** personae to describe himself at times. No ambiverts here! Florestan ≈ extroverted, while Eusebius ≈ introverted. This poem catches an essence.

The next few poems live in the genre of comedy and absurdity. And so, in this true fashion, I present the **Hermes And Icarus** poem! Just for a moment imagine how silly the conversation might become if these two were to meet. Anybody listening might think they are fruit 'n' nut cases!

And now, we've reached the point that you've all been waiting for: the return of Mr Spock. By popular demand he's back. What havoc could he be creating onboard the Starship Second Prize, now! The poem **Mr Spock Finds Cupid's Bow And Arrow** gives you some idea what could be going on in outer space.

Blow, You Icy Windy! is a contrary poem. It is perfect for those mid-winter days — not! By the end you will be longing to move in with the frozen peas! And, while you are greatly looking forward to this — if not demanding it — I have chosen just the right piece of music! N.B. Chronologically speaking, it was the last to be written for this collection.

At university I studied Photomedia. For the Degree Show I decided to photograph church buildings, cut the photographs into triangles and arrange them in squares — all by hand. Once I had completed framing them, they were ready for the end-of-course exhibition. These finished, square pieces were termed 'quadratures'. That was in 2004. In 2021 I wrote the poem **The Ode To The Quadrature.**

The poem **Checkmate!** is about the game of chess — particularly, the Queen-Bishop attack strategy from beginning to end. If you were to choose a piece of music to match this tactical game, what would be your choice? My suggestion is at the back of the book. Incidentally, I recorded the piece on my piano. The five-beats-to-the-bar time signature has been known to unsettle.

The **Summer Wind** poem in this book is a companion to the Summer Rain poem from my first poetry book. Once again there is music, dance and special treats. The weather is enchantingly efficacious in the way it transcends normal and expected behaviour. The whole poem is beautiful, rich and satisfying. The secret: the couple's mind: love.

Have you ever come across a poem with philosophical content? **The Old, Wise Philosopher** prose poem is a basic and fundamental enquiry. And here is the first stanza:

There once was an old, wise philosopher who asked:
"*Is* there such a thing as a thing…?"
He read and read
And thought and thought
And concluded:
"Yes, there is such a thing as a thing"

And now a few words about the images in this book. They are all photographs of church buildings that have been manipulated in photo-editing software to produce geometric abstract designs in black and white. Each image has a characteristic serif as a signature.

And so to the music. Music is a passion. At some stage of my poetry, from composition through to audio and/or video productions, ideas of compatible music effortlessly surfaces to my consciousness. An example of threshold mental activity in some cases may approximate:

Poem: **The Myth Of The Tara Brooch**
Celtic music
Music from the past
Musical instruments from the past
Music related to themes of the poem
What does the music evoke?
What does the music bring to the poem?
Do I have the musical score on my shelf?

Ultimately, I rely on the 'feel right' factor.

"Finally, brothers, whatever is true, whatever is honourable, whatever is just, whatever is pure, whatever is lovely, whatever is commendable, if there is any excellence, if there is anything worthy of praise, think about these things "

Philippians 4:8 (ESV)

The Myth Of The Tara Brooch

Be fearful of the intricate Tara Brooch
Especially the wearer on your approach
Made of gold, silver and electrum
And precious stones from colours' spectrum
Once worn by aristocratic poet warrior
The indomitable, undefeated Queen Boudicca

The Tara Brooch imparts superpowers
That remains on wearer for untold hours
Transforming eyes into preying kestrel's
Able to see elements invisible
And roaring, ferocious sabre-toothed jaws
Defeating Merlin with single roars

Presently waiting Tara Brooch domiciled
Back in native Emerald Isle
Her location guarded, secret
Watching for malevolent zealots
When such megalomaniacs appear
She will be adorned — full square!

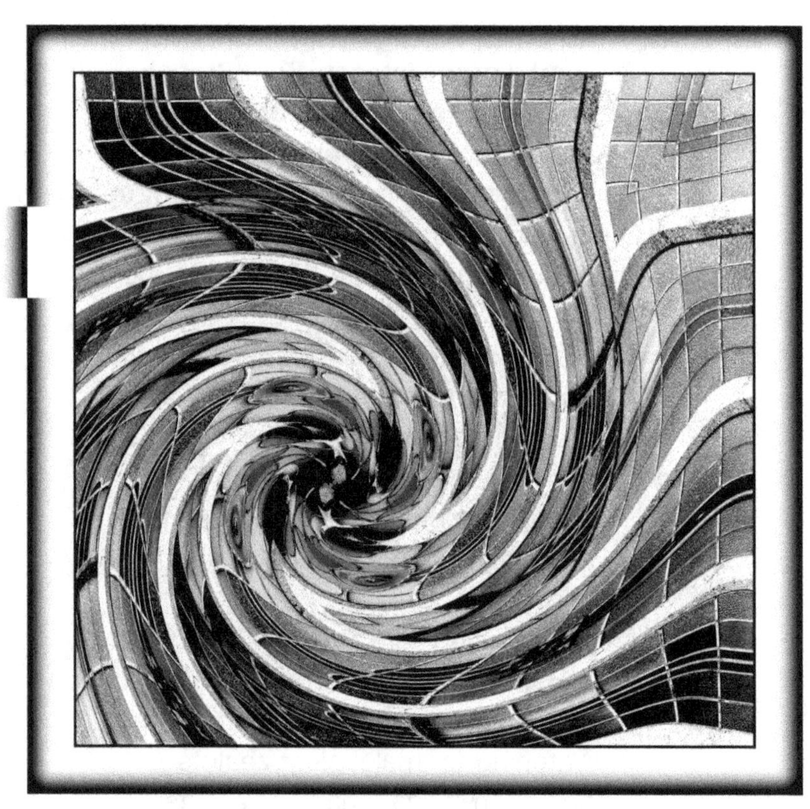

Bromley Common Methodist Church

Good Morning

Early in the morning
The dawn chorus is deafening
And nothing else is heard
No other creature is stirred

The clean, fresh air
Is what the morning wears
And the day's first light
Is quite gentle and light

The whole morning atmosphere
Is unique and very rare
Yet arrives every day
Promising fruit like faye

It is impossible to quench
What the five senses sense
Whatever they detect
Enjoy, do not neglect

Passers-by in the morning
Exchange a joyful greeting
Smiling as they toot
Like melodies on a flute

Good Afternoon

I've just finished lunch
And decide to invite some friends over
It's impromptu, and all very cordial
Minutes later guests start arriving at leisure

There's a warm breeze in the air
And I top up the ice buckets
The sundial looks happy today
Everyone is relaxed and contented

Smiles and laughter accompanies conversation
Life is good, free and easy...
As the party naturally closes
One guest serenades another on the guitar

Good Night

The sun slowly sets
Beneath the distant horizon
Today, a thousand memories were made
Special, every one

As I gaze out from the tower
I see Abraham's children — the stars above
Resembling the children on the beach
The grains of sand filled with The Dove

Sunflowers know not where to look
The eye's iris radial muscles shrink back
All the colours of the rainbow
Now not singing like the lark

Contemplating in the rocking chair
No longer rocking to and fro
I rise and play a Chopin Nocturne
On the Pleyel grand piano

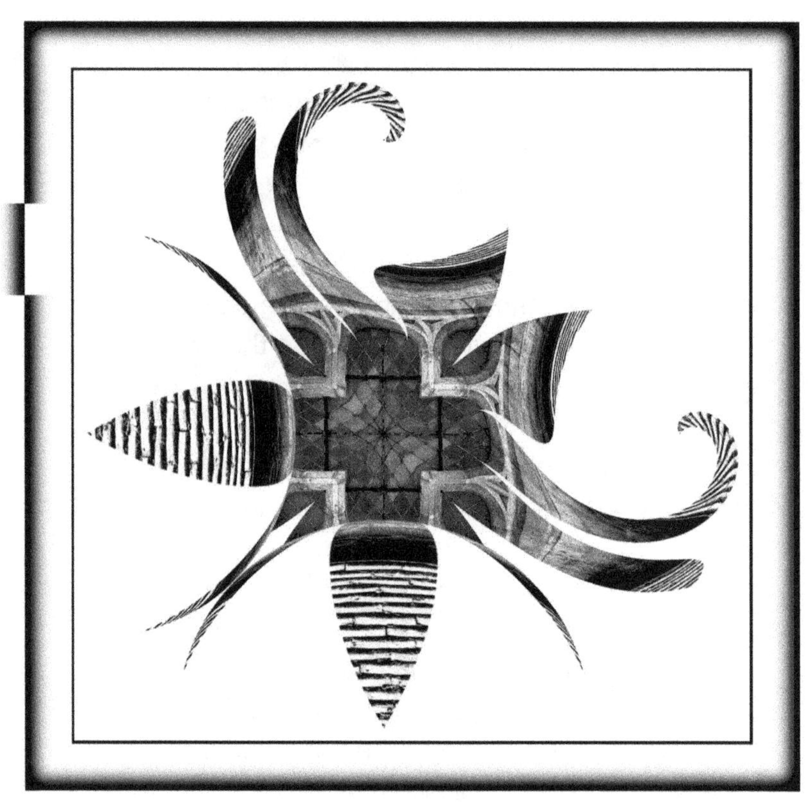

Bromley Parish Church

If Only I Could Dream

If only I could dream
I would dream of...
Riding the spacetime continuum
Be home before I left
Finish writing this poem
before writing the first word
And experience life
before it began

If only I could dream
I would dream of...
Wearing high end tailored clothes
that were fine and distinctive
Hats that would set one apart
And shoes that carried a royal warrant

If only I could dream
I would dream of...
Breakfast with a view
where the scenery is spectacular
at the top of the tallest
Or beneath the ocean
in a luxury cruise submarine
Or onboard an exclusive spacecraft

	If only I could dream
	I would dream of...
Dinner with the Saints of yesteryear
reclining and feasting till satisfied
Listening to the sages of the ages
discussing the world's mysteries
...and laughing together
until The Man upstairs descends
to join the party

	If only I could dream
	I would dream of...
Tea with the love of my life
I would look into her eyes
and she into mine
Engage profound communication
Sometimes words cannot express

	If only I could dream
	I would dream of...
A mutual fall into love
Complimenting each other's compliments
Compatible to the nth
A reciprocating reciprocal
Discovering and creating dimensions
exclusive to the fugue of matrimony

	If only I could dream
	I would dream of...
Living on an island
with my darling wife
One hundred miles from the nearest neighbour
Just the three of us
or would that be five?
Well, after all, the Trinity is three-in-one

If only I could dream
I would dream of...
A more intimate relationship with God
To be like the Holy Spirit
and search His deep thoughts
To experience and live
in the third heaven
every millisecond of every day

If only I could dream
I would dream of...
Dreaming more until I could dream
Dreaming less until I could dream

If only

If only I could dream

If only I could dream
I would dream of...
...dreaming

The Maiden's Dream

...Softing, softing peaches, cream
Pastel colours forever seen
Softing, softing peaches, cream
Juicy nectar sweetest clean

Horsing, horsing galloping beach
Waves advancing onward leap
Horsing, horsing galloping beach
Backward never, never creep

Softing, softing petals fall
Falling ever purist flower
Softing, softing petals fall
Falling lilies fall forever

Knighting, knighting white charger
Kissing, caressing, loving, tender
Knighting, knighting white charger
Cannot bear dreaded asunder

Mooning, mooning flashes light
Carriage waiting, hero gone
Mooning, mooning flashes light
Time painful, hurting, long

Softing, softing lyre tune
Longing poetry, longing hand
Softing, softing lyre tune
Melody from forgotten land

Softing, softing candle light
Comforting castle's lonely soul
Softing, softing candle light
Lighting hero's armour gold

Horsing, horsing hero comes
Drawbridge closes, warmer weather
Horsing, horsing hero comes
Kissing, caressing, loving, tender

Crusting, crusting sparkling crown
Carbon earth intensely crushed
Crusting, crusting sparkling crown
Foreign kings forever hushed

Hairing, hairing posies plenty
Dancing merrily, dancing free
Hairing, hairing posies plenty
Lyre playing happy melody

Sleeping maiden gently wakens
Leaving dreamland's playing ground
Turning softly under covers
Wearing diamond crusted crown

Tick-Tock, Tick-Tock

Tick-tock, tick-tock
The hands go round
They never stop

Tick-tock, tick-tock
Get out the bed
Get out the cot

Tick-tock, tick-tock
Make le-mon tea
2 lumps; plop plop

Tick-tock, tick-tock
Jump in the car
Hop hop, hop hop

Tick-tock, tick-tock
The traffic crawls
I want to rock!

Tick-tock, tick-tock
Once at my desk
The phone rings hot

Tick-tock, tick-tock
The boss is wrong
Don't knock, don't knock

Tick-tock, tick-tock
The sandwich's warm
The coffee's not

Tick-tock, tick-tock
The meeting's long
I want to pop!

Tick-tock, tick-tock
Late back from work
Fed up, fed up

Tick-tock, tick-tock
Plant kiss on wife
Drink slop, drink slop

Tick-tock, tick-tock
Fall into bed
Fall into cot

Tick-tock, tick-tock
The hands go round
They never stop

Tick-tock, tick-tock
Get out the bed
Get out the cot

Tick-tock, tick-tock
Make le-mon tea
Two lumps; plop plop

Tick-tock, tick

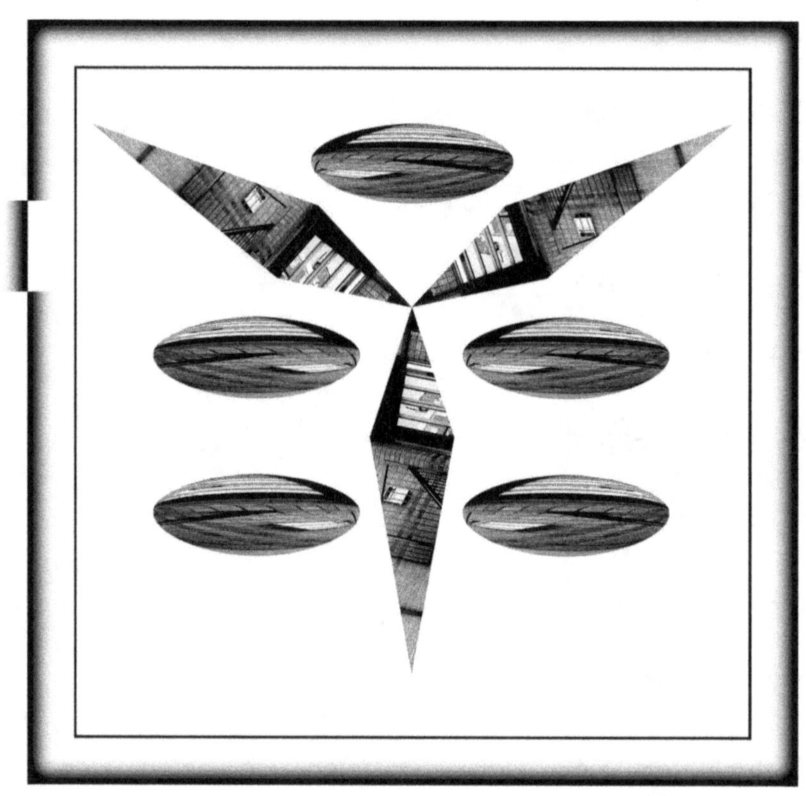

Christ Church Anerley

It Must Have Taken Hours And Hours

It must have taken hours and hours
For God to make the beautiful flowers
Their natural colours are yellow, red and green
With petals so soft and bright and clean

All they need is sunshine and water
To make sure they grow better
And flying creatures to pollinate
At their own exceedingly natural rate

High Shone The Shining Sun

High shone the shining sun
Playing in it is such fun
It shone all day
In merry, merry May
And made me want to skip and run

The Heavens Are Full Of Stars

The heavens are full of stars
And planets like Jupiter and Mars
They shine all night
As bright as white light
And have other interesting particulars

Bumble-Bee

Bumble, bumble, bumble-bee
Buzzing to flower and to tree
Then back to the hive
And does a little jive
Making honey for you and for me

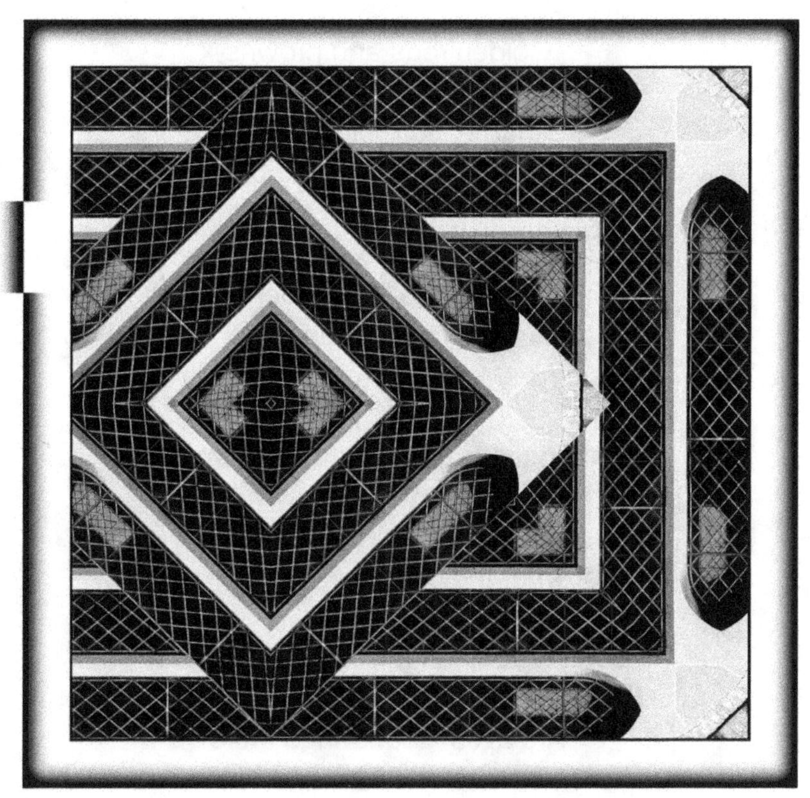

Christ Church Beckenham

Feathers (Part 1)

Golden reds and browns
The season is turning
Ruddy and rustic colours
The deciduous is changing

Abscission triggered by hormones
Earth welcomes the detachments
Autumn is upon us
Discarded transformed into nutrients

Among the brushwood and brambles
There are fruit and flowers and seeds
And other shedded parts
Just what the growing season needs

But lying still on the woodland's floor
All fallen, all forlorn
Are aves' abandoned attire
This November at day's dawn

At this time and hour
I can be found in such a place
Breathing in clean air
And walking at gentle pace

However, on this particular occasion
My awareness became lit
The atmosphere was somehow different
Cannot quite put my finger on it

There was a kind of static electricity
Spread horizontally in the air
Lower than the tops of trees
Like a mist hanging there

Then, all of a sudden
A whirlwind stirs the charge
Nothing else is touched or moves
Whether small, medium or large

Flickering lights then appear
And touch aves' abandoned attire
Each then burst into life
Flashing like new fire

Then, one by one
Before unprepared eyes
They are transformed
Into maidens beautified

I try to count them
Two, five, seven
Could this somehow be
A revelation from heaven?

I try to count again
Eleven, six, no three
Their number keeps changing
Away, be gone futility!

They run and jump
And skip and fly
Smile and beckon me
To have a wilful try

My efforts to emulate
Were not very good
That fresh, fresh morn
In the wild, wild wood

Then one beautified maiden
Blows a trumpet bright
That sounded like an anthem
All mellifluous, all light

We all began
To dance and twirl
Spinning and weaving
In a merry, merry whirl

Sometimes we danced
In squares or rounds
Sometimes on branches
Sometimes on the ground

We danced and danced
And chanced a chance
To prance and prance
From nuance to nuance

…Then, to my surprise
I hear a cuckoo cuckooing
Is it now the growing season
And we have danced into spring?

No more the sound
Of rustling dry leaves
And falling temperatures
That the autumn conceives

Instead, there are hues
Of vibrant blue, yellow and green
The season has changed
Winter no longer seen

Since last November morn
Had I not realised?
I had been dancing every day
With maidens beautified

Feathers (Part 2)

Then one beautified maiden
Takes me by the hand
I look into her expressions
And see a glorious xand

Gently, gently I am lead
Ever deeper into the wood
The other beautified maidens
Continue in their rood

In whiteness we tread on
On no particular path
Sometimes our hands parted
Sometimes our hands clasped

Sometimes the beautified maiden
Turns and radiates at me
Sometimes she gracefully dances
Around every other tree

Deeper and wilder
The forest becomes
Thicker and greener
The way abounds

It is now that I hear
The trickling of a stream
And smell the lush flora
As freshly scented green

As we continue in the woodland
Which I consider Arcadian
The trickling stream becomes a rush
Delighting the beautified maiden

I look on and forward
Through ever greener glades
And see a broadened clearing
Where hangs a misty haze

When we reach the broadened clearing
I see a magnificent sight
A thunderous sunlit waterfall
And a rainbow coloured bright

Then the beautified maiden
Smiles and takes my hand
We fly through the air at speed
No longer touching the ground

We are heading for the waterfall
And plunge into its torrent
Passing through we emerge
But are not even wet

My eyes twinkle a millisecond
We are now in a different dimension
Static electric charges randomly appear
Just like cold atomic fission

Ten thousand times ten thousand
Feathered, beautified maidens
Are dancing and playing freely
Adorned with garlands Arcadian

My eyes twinkle yet again
And I see a land deified
With ten thousand times ten thousand
More feathered maidens beautified

There is music everywhere
That I had never, ever heard
Emanating from a central source
Interlaced with words upon words

The merry, feathered, beautified maidens
In direct relation to the central source
Danced and played and twirled and twirled
Of course. Of course. Of course!

Determined to see the source
As close as close can be
I pressed passed the maidens
To see what I could see

All words grow pale
When held against this source
And in the drawing close
All experience is put in reverse

No, not even that, I say
I, myself, is transformed
Becoming light as a feather
And only appear forlorn

So, whenever the wind comes and goes
The air is somehow changed
Static electricity flashes to and fro
And my attention is engaged

Then, this is the time to play
To hop, skip, jump and go
To dance in ancient forest
To blow the bright trumpet, blow

To take another's hand
And to gently, gently lead
To streams and wondrous fonts
In the middle of a wooded mead

Listen to the seasons
Smell the wooded water
Enjoy every shade and hue
Smile and make much laughter

I hear the warbling birdsong
I smell the scented flower
I see the double rainbow
I feel the touch of a feather

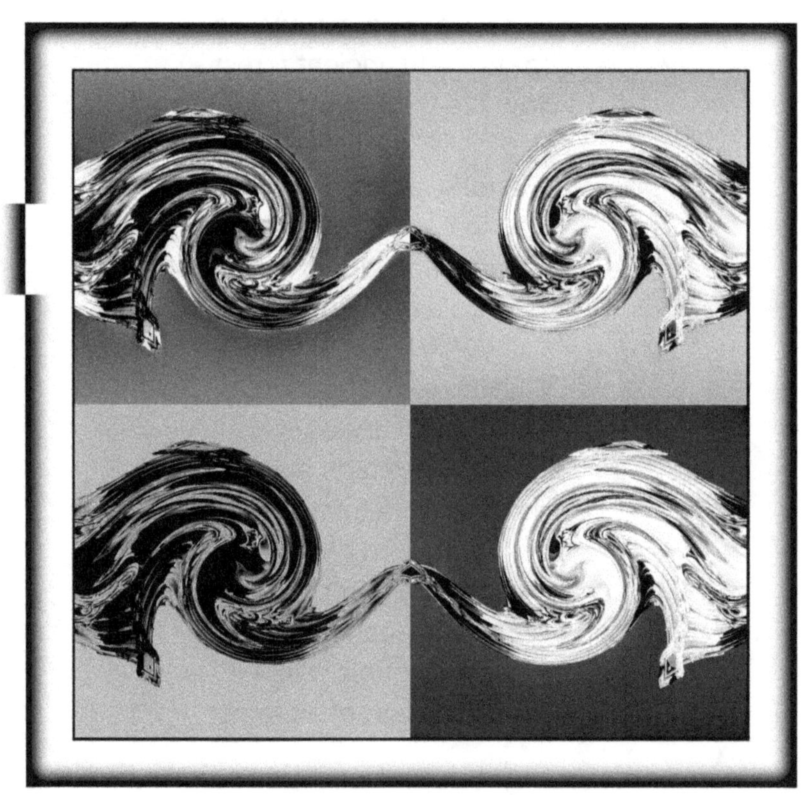

Christ Church Gypsy Hill 1

The Cairns Of Ingleborough

The stony cairns of Ingleborough
Keeps calling me to themselves
"Come, make the treacherous journey
Ascend the mountain's shelves"

They whisper from long ago
They whisper ten hundred furlongs
Their whisper is strong and sure
Their whisper is like a song

"Make haste and come to us
Ignore the point of no return
The marshy bog will not swallow
Burn your bridges, burn"

Though the precipitous mountainside
Is raw, rough and rugged
And dangers await every move
On shelves narrow and jagged

I press on and upwards
Only slipping now and again
Climbing on hands and knees
Ignoring any muscular pain

I keep fixed in my mind
The cairns whisper and call
That I will be stronger
With every slip and fall

Two hours later
I sight the treasured cairns
And all my weaknesses
Shrivels up and burns

My energy is multiplied
Every scratch and fissure forgotten
All my ineffectiveness disappears
Because they are now rotten

Just another hundred yards
That's all I have to commit
To reach the plateaued top
To reach Ingleborough's summit

Beholding the cairns of Ingleborough
Was absolutely thrilling
And looking down at the scenery
…Then, it started raining!

My Everyday Oban

The cock crows…
sending defused points
of light through early mist
that reflects in the still waters
of bonny Oban Bay

…At half and 12 noon
a wee bonny lass
stands on the ruins of Dunollie Castle
piping to the heavy ferries
sailing to Argyle's isles

…Near the end of the day
I view a spectacular sunset
from high on McCaig's Tower…
One thousand cameras go 'click'
and I chat to a kilted local

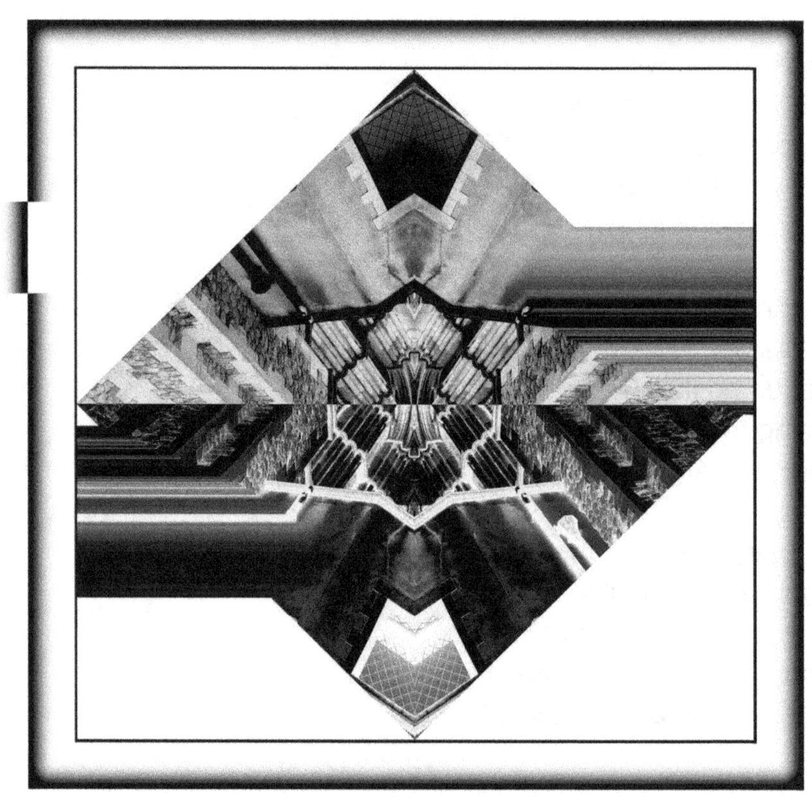

Christ Church Gypsy Hill 2

She

She has, I would say
    An air of confidence
    Standing so, so tall
    With a height so small

She radiates, I would say
    The power of deep blue
    Without speaking a word
    Her voice can be heard

She has, I would say
    The look of an executive
    Every movement exact
    Every thought on track

She radiates, I would say
    Professionalism unlimited
    Characterful everywhere
    Repaying the atmosphere

These Words Are By Far Few

These words are by far few
To express what is long overdue
Time and time and time again
I have struggled to contain

But now I have reached the stage
To put my experience on page
As I no longer lead you astray
Some of which you have guessed before today

You have known me as a friend
And you wish that, that will never end
But there are tons and miles more
To what I have in store

There are times when I think of you
And, oh, if only you knew
How my heart begins to race
To a greatly accelerated pace

And I feel so deep inside
There are few places to run and hide
So please, put an end to my strive
Allow me to give you abundant life

There is much more to be gained
A higher level to be obtained
A duet of harmony and pleasure
A feast to enjoy and treasure

Possess life in all its fullness
Grasp goodness, success and progress
With God at the centre of us two
Making hopes and dreams come true

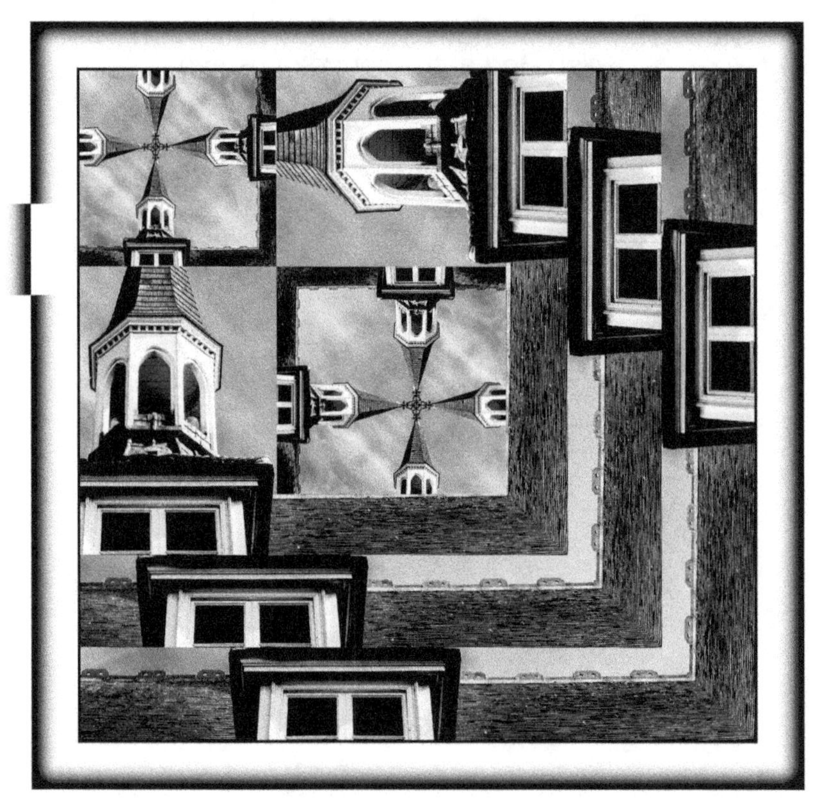

Christ Church Bromley 1

The Armour Of GOD

Finally, after being blessed with every spiritual blessing
And much, much prayer and much, much thanksgiving
Be transformed so you are sensitive to Christ
Be united with Him and live His life first
Be united in His body and keep it tight
Living as offspring of pure white light
Wives and husbands follow the Good Book
And children to your parents you must look

Stand, after relinquishing worldviews and paradigms
Which will never satiate any human mind
Because they take reality and then rearrange
Don't vacillate, by definition reality does not change
You know that reality and truth are observable
God's truth is one hundred percent provable
Truth is always true for everyone everywhere
Truth is always true in every heavenly sphere

Stand tall and upright with fortified emotion
Worthless the righteousness derived from man's notion
God is the one who makes us righteous
We can never do it, we are just pompous
God is the one who freely justifies
Grace and mercy from heaven He flies
God declares it over your life
So put an end to all your strife

Stand firm with your willing and beautiful feet
Set an extra place next time you eat
Imagine you are entertaining the Prince of peace
Invite everyone to dine and enjoy the feast
Be ready to share the reconciliation plan
With the young and the old and every man
God's great gospel: peace towards men
For every stranger, for every friend

Take your belief in the Holy Scripture
Which evil can never, ever, puncture
Hide in the shadow of this shield
Then spiritual attacks will be repealed
In all the firing and flaming of the arrow
Take heart, they will be quenched tomorrow
This piece of armour is in addition
(Now, where did I put that mountain!)

Think about the whole process of salvation
Justification, sanctification and glorification
Think about the Holy Spirit who is present continuous
Simultaneously dwelling in heaven and within us
Think about Him, He is the Two Edged Sword
He is God and The Mystery of God's Word
For the Holy Spirit is a person
One of the three persons in one

And pray in the spirit on all occasions
With all kinds of prayers and supplications
Be quick to notice what is unusual
And anything that has a dangerous potential
Keep on praying for all the saints
Pray continuously, and you, do not faint

Be strong in the Lord and in his mighty power
Wear God's comfortable armour hour by hour

The Lion Of Judah

Who is this King standing tall and square
Banishing His enemies with a single stare
Every creature will fall to its knees
And some will beg: "Please, Lord, please!"
Others will raise their hands in honest praise
And worship the wondrous Ancient of Days

His eyes are like furious, flaming fire
Consuming what His Father desires
Decisively dividing sheep from goats
His songs of judgement have piercing notes
Are you on the left or right?
Make sure you are standing in the light

He rides out on a pure white horse
Steadfast and strong throughout the course
Multiple crowns upon His head
His robe dipped in blood ruby red
Leading His finely dressed legions of angels
Into every corner of every realm

His tongue projects striking nations and all
Penetrating deep dividing spirit and soul
On His robe and thigh are written the words
KING OF KINGS AND LORD OF LORDS
Treading the winepress of God's wrath
His enemies cannot escape His path

Work out your salvation with fear and trembling
Because, you know not what tomorrow brings
In all your hearing please be observant
Listening for: "Well done good and faithful servant"
But if your sins are not burned through
Your ears will hear: "Away from me, I never knew you!"

But God knows the little ones and sets us apart
Setting eternity deep into our hearts
His Holy Spirit whispers in His unique way
That we will be married on that Special Day
Christ Jesus who fills the entire universe
Will return for us His beloved Church

The Ecstasy Of Hildegard

Spiritual, spiritual heavenly pure
Benedictine abbess is sure, is sure
Historical time is high Middle Ages
Sacred monophony not bound to pages
Catholic emotions excited, free
Convent's dynamic, ecstatic melody

Holy Doctor of the Church
Search: Hildegard of Bingen, search
The shade of the living light fills her eye
Inspiring the faithful to draw nigh
Resonating, reverberating, contrast, drama
Her visions make nothing of human strata

"God's love, God's love," heralds angeline
To prototypical Sibyl of the Rhine
His arrow is swift and better than best
Piercing perishable, temporal flesh
His love is better than life itself
She cries:
"Take me, heavenly Mother, to Yourself"

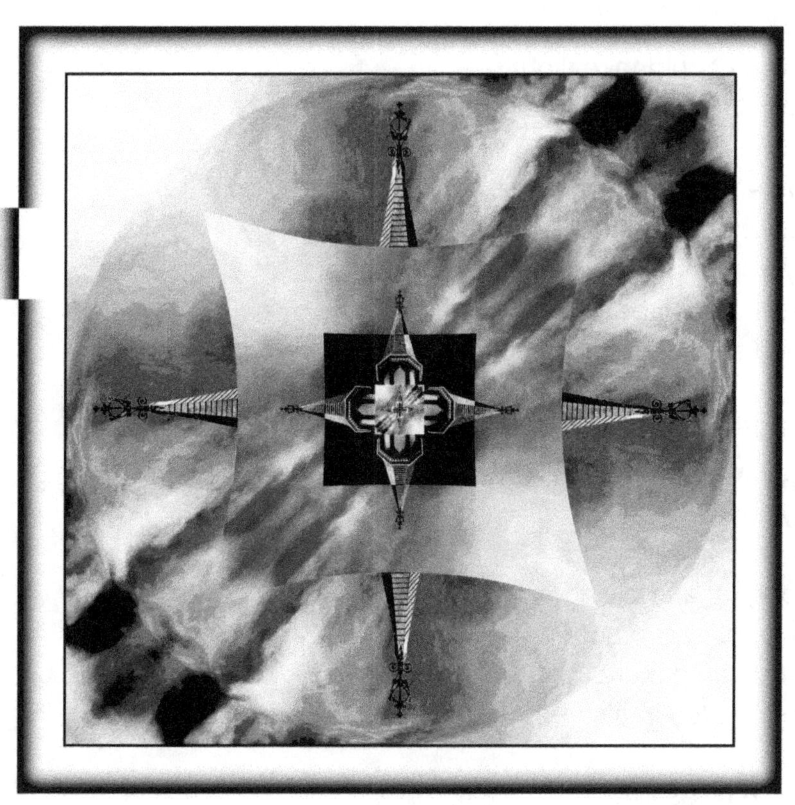

Christ Church Bromley 2

I Wish I Was A Kite

I wish I could take flight
Into clouds fluffy white
Exercising my ability
To defy magnetic gravity
No longer held and bound
By trappings of the ground
Much, much better
Than solid terra firma

I wish I was a kite
Achieving great height
Flying so high
In heaven's first sky
Dodging and diving
Swooping and soaring
Or hanging there
Suspended in air

I wish I was like
An ejected stalagmite
Or absolutely anything
That is on a wing
Like a flying aeroplane
But without the window pane
Like a flying fish
Not landing on a dish

I wish I was a preying kyte
Searching for something to bite
As quick as an avian hunter
Selecting vertebrates like a predator
Employing great vision
In a single mission
To swoop on prey
From a long way away

I wish I flew the Dolomites
Gasping at the Alpen sights
Either Western or Little
Eyes not knowing where to settle
Slowly, slowly drifting
Higher and higher lifting
On the thermals of noon
In a hot air balloon

I wish I owned a skyward trike
With jet engines to ignite
Two attached on either side
Reaching Mach 2 in the ride
Slowing down homeward bound
1,000 feet before the ground
Parachutes automatically deploy
Welcoming landlubbers with a, "ahoy!"

I wish I could the sky excite
Like a comet in the night
Blazing the solar system
As regular as a rhythm
Hurtling across outer space
Aimless and at a pace
Daring to dare a dare
Scratching Earth's atmosphere

I wish I was a heavenly spright
Only *just* out of sight
Beings ancient and old
Guarding the human soul
Crying: "Holy, holy, holy
Is the Lord God Almighty!"
Celestial and supernatural
Executing God's will

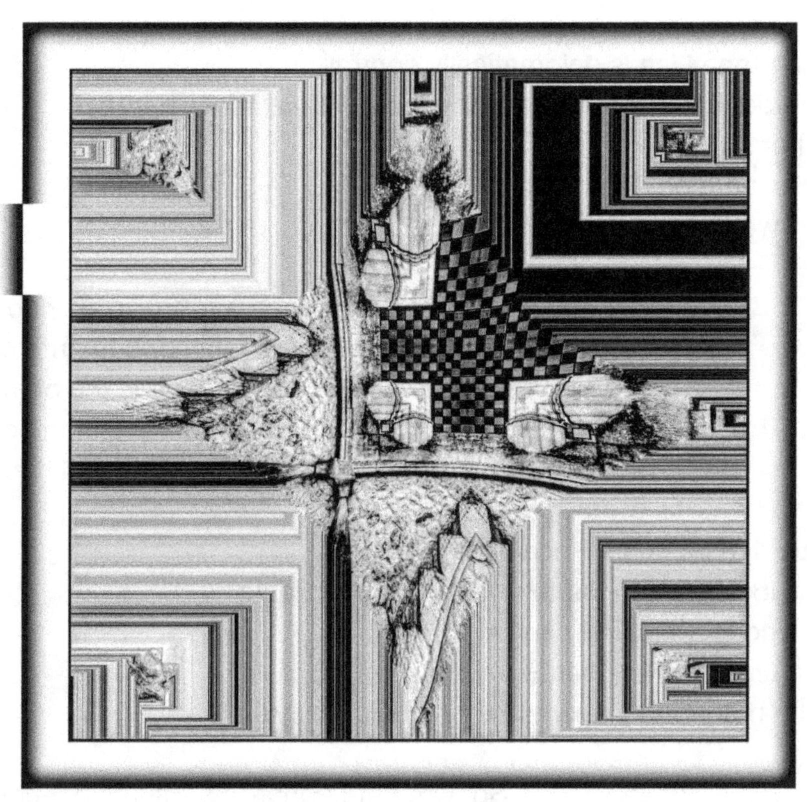

Greek Orthodox Church, Upper Norwood

Leonardo da Vinci 1452-1519

The Mona Lisa is enigmatically contrary
Embodying opposing characteristics simultaneously
Is her smile engaging?
Or is it a mocking?
Will we ever unravel human complexity!?

The Last Supper is a simple composition
Depicting a varied display of human emotion
Which one is the betrayer?
But... all serene in the centre
Sits Jesus in this sequential narration

Vitruvian Man is a Renaissance symbol
The ideal human inside shapes irreconcilable
The concept is first century BC
But drawn by Leonardo da Vinci
Who made the ancient theory iconic and visible

So, what of Leonardo's visual appearance?
Is the red chalk drawing a true resemblance?
To say it is a self-portrait
Some scholars would rather faint
Because age sixty-seven he retired from existence!

Florestan And Eusebius

The Florestan in me
grins, showing all the teeth
The Eusebius in me
turns up the corners of the mouth
Lips gently pursed together

The Florestan in me
opens the eyes wide
The Eusebius in me
lowers the eyebrows
taking in everything with a blink

The Florestan in me
greets with a big hug
The Eusebius in me
shakes hands
and says: "How do you do?"

The Florestan in me
parts, saying: "See you soon"
The Eusebius in me
says: "Goodbye," and
"Have a safe journey"

The Florestan in me
is an R.E.M. dreamer
The Eusebius in me
daydreams, engaging
somewhat beautiful pensivity

The Florestan in me
sits at the piano
and plays a Chopin ballade
The Eusebius in me
sits at the piano
and plays a Chopin ballade

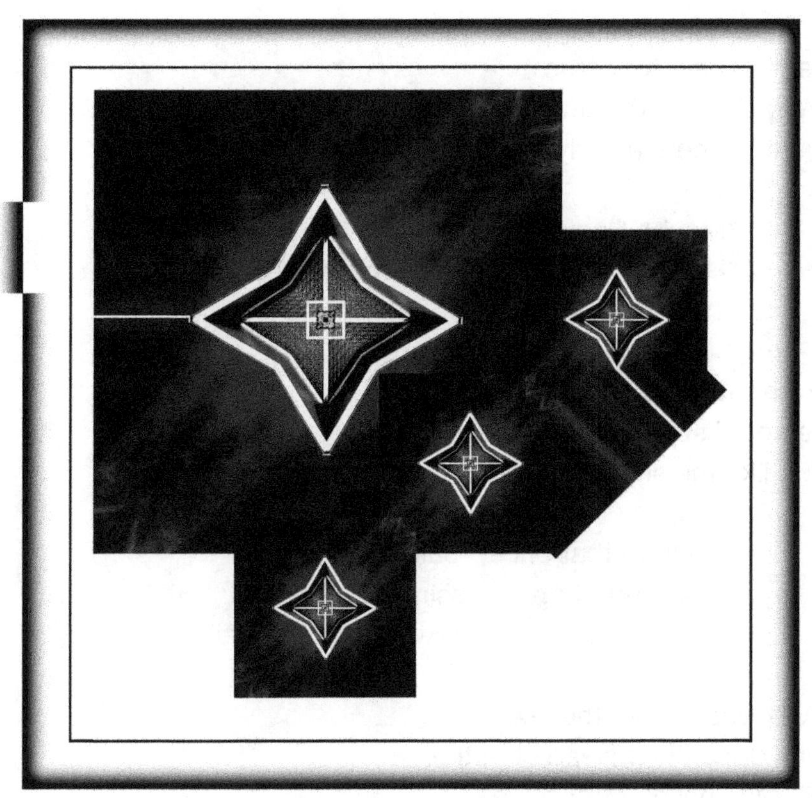

St Paul's Church, Crystal Palace 1

Hermes And Icarus

Hermes said to Icarus
"Why doesn't the duck-billed platypus
Have feathers and fly in the sky?"

    "Maybe," said Icarus
    "He thinks flying is far too much fuss
    Then again, I think he's too lazy to try"

"What about the ostrich
He could step off a high-rise ledge
Just like the skyscraper in uptown Dubai?"

    "He tried that once," said Icarus
    "And landed on a passing Airbus
    Which took him all the way to Shanghai"

"And what about the kiwi
Why doesn't he sleep on a tree
Or wave hello or goodbye?"

    "That's something to do
    With his Great Grandfather called Chom-Chew
    Who cut off his wings and made fruit pie"

    Then Icarus said to Hermes
    "You can guess why dodos use a trapeze
    Guesstimations at 5:15 are fine"

“That's absolutely ludicrous”
Said Hermes to Icarus
“I can't even tell the time!”

Mr Spock Finds Cupid's Bow And Arrow

Chilled Champagne and sautéed beef
Why put it off until tomorrow?
Today is February 14th!
Mr Spock finds Cupid's bow and arrow

Mr Spock's secret imagination
Entertains the love he could create
Between Captain Kirk and Mademoiselle Klingon
Holding hands on their first date

"I can see the day when they are wed"
Mr Spock continues to think
"Captain Kirk kissing the Klingon's head
Then vomits in the sink"

How can Monsieur Klingon put to flight
The longings in his heart to prove
He cries himself to sleep every night
Desperate for intergalactic love

So Mr Spock does not hesitate
And loosens the arrow from his hand
Transforming Uhura into the Klingon's mate
There's a twinkling in the eye of that woman

The next time he is beamed on board
She will kiss him on his bony head
And he will be flopping like a pup
And stop taking the anti-depression meds

Treaties are made between galaxies
When aliens find a mate
Love is stronger than tractor beams
In that futuristic star date

Just another day on the Starship Second Prize
Tomorrow's episode promises more
As they continue on their great commission:
"To boldly celebrate love like never before!"

Blow, You Icy Windy!

Blow, you icy windy blow, blow, Blow!
Bring us Frost and bring us snow, snow, snow
Bring us Frozen, icy bergs, bergs, bergs
Blow, you icy windy blow, blow, Blow!

Go Away you hot and sunny sun, sun, sun
You are No More welcome better run, run, Run

Come Now freezing weather come, come, come
Minus Fahrenheit is much more Fun, Fun, Fun
Just to roll about in snow, snow, Snow
Come Now freezing weather come, come, come

Just to slip and slide about is Great, Great, Great
Me and chill burns are best mates, mates, mates
Frozen Toes and frozen Nose, nose, nose
Quickly, Jack Frost, Don't be late, late, late

Blow, you icy windy blow, blow, Blow!
Bring us Frost and bring us snow, snow, snow
Bring us Frozen, icy bergs, bergs, bergs
Blow, you icy windy blow, blow, BLOW!

…don't you just love blizzards

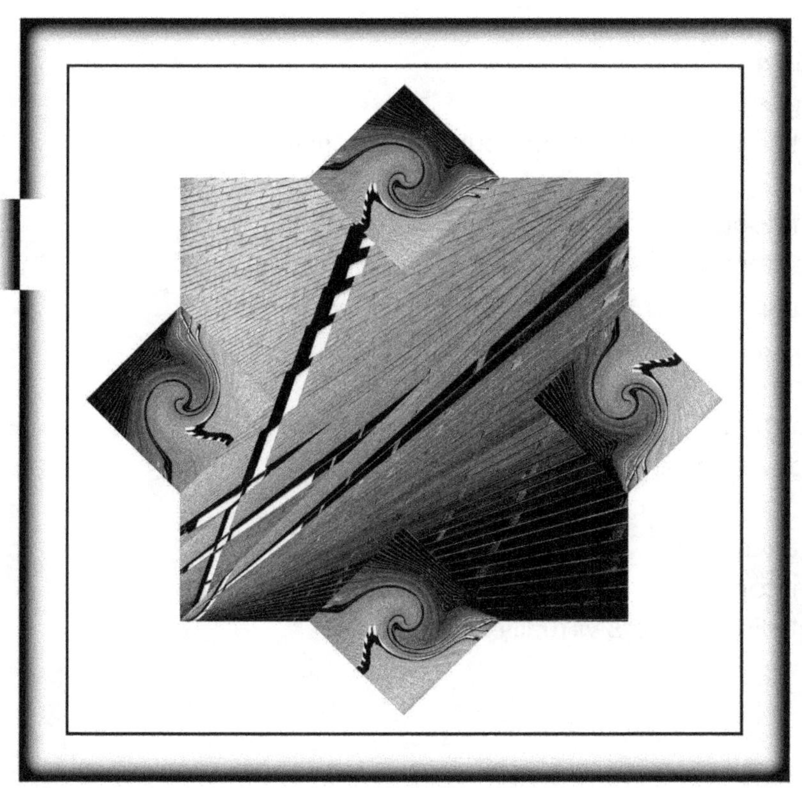

South Norwood Baptist Church

Ode To The Quadrature

Fugal
Digital
Artistically constructed counterpoint, fine

Photographic
Geometric
Sample the graphic design

Elementary
Harmony
Conventional kaleidoscope couldn't hold

Architecture
Photomedia
Building aspects virtually controlled

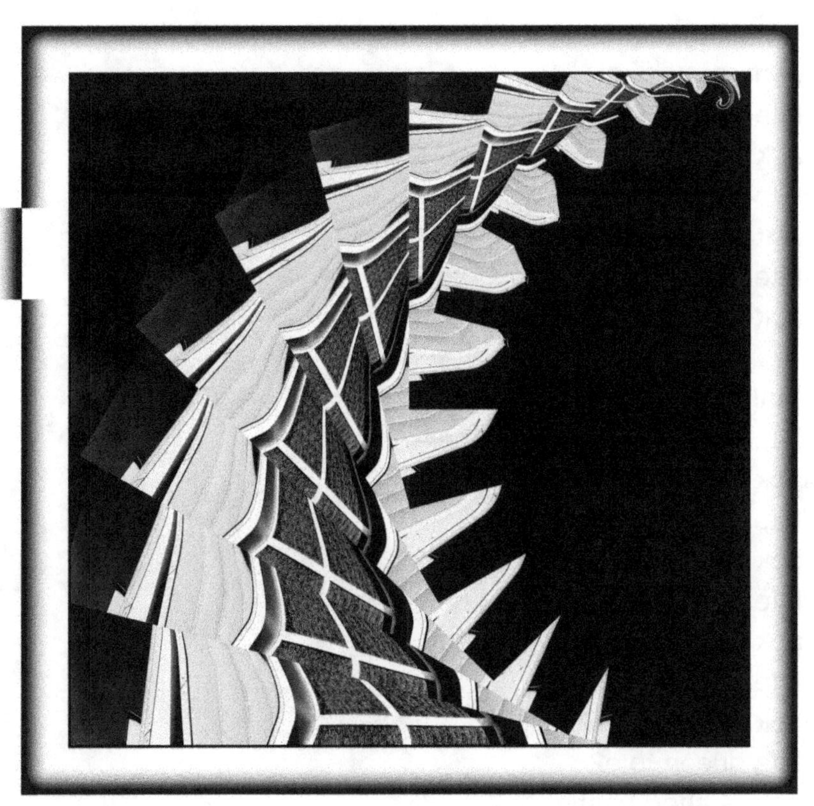

St Paul's Church, Crystal Palace 2

Checkmate! The Queen-Bishop Attack

Opening:
White pawn to e4
Black pawn e6
White pawn to d4
Black pawn to d5
White knight to c3
Black pawn takes pawn on e4

Middle Game:
White knight takes pawn on e4
Black knight to d7
White knight to f3
Black knight on file g to f6
White knight takes knight on f6 – check
Black knight takes knight on f6
White bishop to d3
Black bishop to e7
White queen to e2
Black — short castle
White bishop to g5
Black pawn to 6 (bad move)

Endgame:
White bishop takes knight on f6
Black bishop takes bishop on f6
White queen to e4
Black protects attacked rook
Queen takes pawn on h7 – checkmate

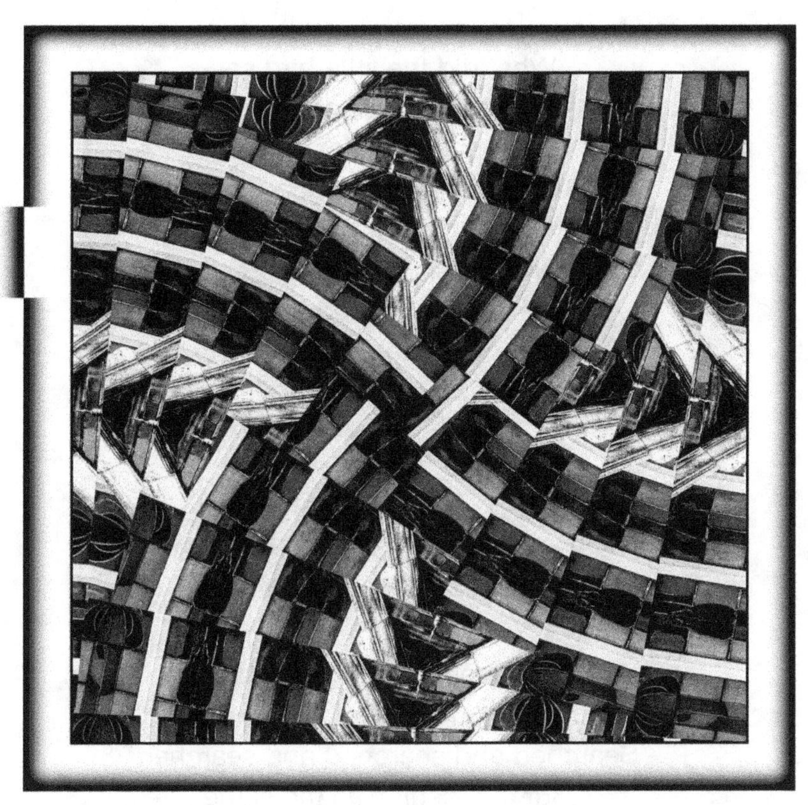

South Norwood URC 1

What Did The Little Bird Say...?

What did the little bird say
As he hopped, hopped, hopped
In the recreation park
On the grassy top, top, top?

On the verdant green grass
He looked, looked, looked
But could not find a worm
To hook, hook, hook

He pecked and pecked
Here and there
Dug and dug
Everywhere!

He hopped to the next patch
And did it again
Searched and searched and searched
But the result was the same

So up he flew
Just like a spring
Chirp, chirping away
On the wing, wing, wing

I am A Dainty Butterfly

I am a dainty butterfly
D'Arcy is my name
I love to flip and flop about
My air dance is never the same

I look like a handkerchief
Being tugged from place to place
And humans try to catch me
In a game of nets 'n' chase

But when I am not flying
I am as docile as docile can be
Opening and closing my wings
Making myself look pretty

I am nature's ornament
Brightening any day
Graceful, delicate and sensitive
Beautifying scenery on the way

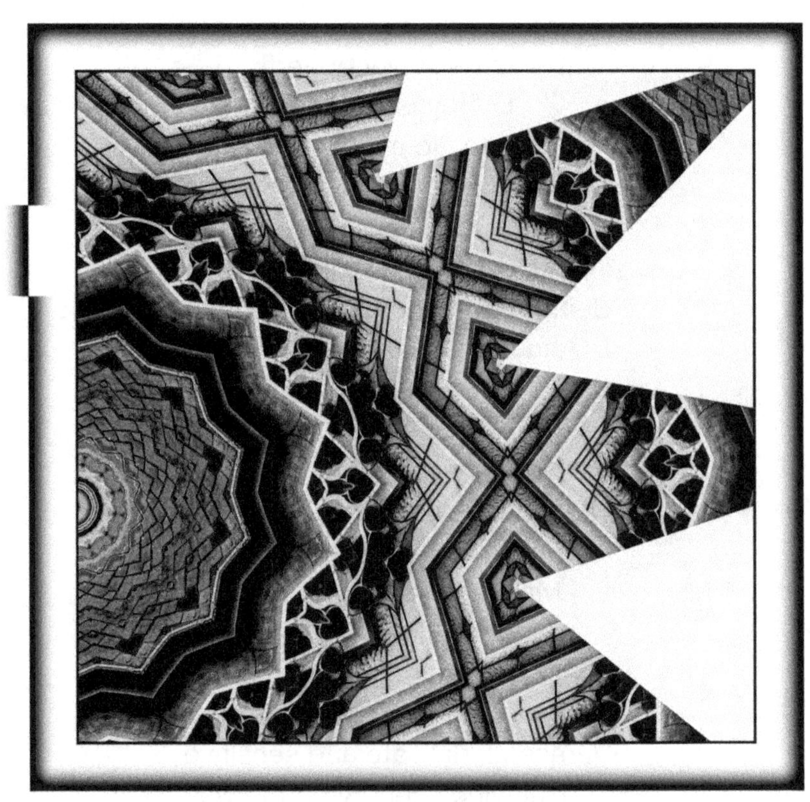

South Norwood URC 2

Summer Wind (with Prologue)

As the butler turned to go
after leaving the pressed morning edition
on the platter beside the bureau
I ask him to prepare afternoon tea

"Certainly," he replies
"But the clock has not struck 11, Sir"

"It is Midsummer's Day
and Madam and I," I explain
"will be having afternoon tea
at the coastal house"

…After an hour
everything is ready
and we begin to make our way

As we leave the grounds
I hear the characteristic buzz and snap
of the motorised electric gate behind us

I look in the rearview mirror
and see the butler's Bentley
I also see the housekeeper on the doorstep
waving us farewell with a handkerchief

As we turn onto the main side road
I ask Madam
who is checking her makeup
on the back seat of our Bentley
to check with the butler
via the two-way communication system
if he had remembered the vinyl records

He replies, "Yes Madam"

—

…As the time reaches two and twenty past
both Bentleys arrive at the coastal house

The standard is raised
and the butler unpacks both cars
including the music

"It is a beautiful day, darling
let us have tea
at the water's edge"
Madam says

"How romantic"
I say

So, after removing our footwear
we carry two chairs and a table down the beach

After setting up next to some rocks
the butler serves us
then retires to a distance
I raise my voice and say to the butler
"Can you bring the record player from the house
and play some music?"

"Yes Sir"

He fetches the player
and puts a record on the turntable
Quite calmly he presses play

The music begins to play

The raised standard once still
begins flapping softly on the mast

Madam stands up
and starts tiptoeing backwards
just as she learned in dance classes
at finishing school

I stand up
turn to her
and start stepping backwards slowly
in true dramatic style

Madam changes direction
and starts tiptoeing towards me

As the music changes
she breaks into a run
And with a leap
she jumps into my arms

I catch her
We embrace sweetly in circular movements
round and round and round

By now the music has become expressive
Expressive, pulsating and undulating

Although it is Midsummer's Day
the clouds are gathering
and the wind is picking up

There are now white pony surfs
but soon they will be white horses

And what of the tide?
Yes, it's advancing
and quicker, too
as if the moon's orbit
was being quickened
by the accelerating music

Then
there is a seventh wave
in time with the orchestra's down bow
and the table and chairs topple over

But we keep with our
ever expressive dance

As the milk and profiteroles
fall to the ground
there is a greater smash of waves
onto the coastal rocks
just as the music reaches a tutti

The water is now rushing our shins
and the
wind whistles wildly…

We part briefly
and, just like ballerinas
raise both arms to form an arch
and pirouette

The music is now at its height

We both grasp each other's left forearm
with our own left hand
right arms still arched in the air

We then look straight and deep
into one another's eyes
and begin an ever-increasing spin

As we spin faster and faster
and look deeper and deeper
into each other's eyes
we are unaware of the tornado
we have created
Or, rather, not us, but the music

We are focused 100% on each other
We are the centre of the whirlwind
everything else is a blur

   …Standard flapping vigorously
   …Cream cakes pulverised
   …Waves pounding rocks
   …Perfuse perspiration pliés

Then, out of nowhere
a white bird descends
down the eye of the whirlwind
and lands calmly on our joined forearms

Our eyes once locked on one another
then looks at the bird
the pure white bird

The moment we do this
the music becomes softer
and our rotation slows down

The whirlwind dissipates…

The butler then approaches and says
"More tea, Sir?"

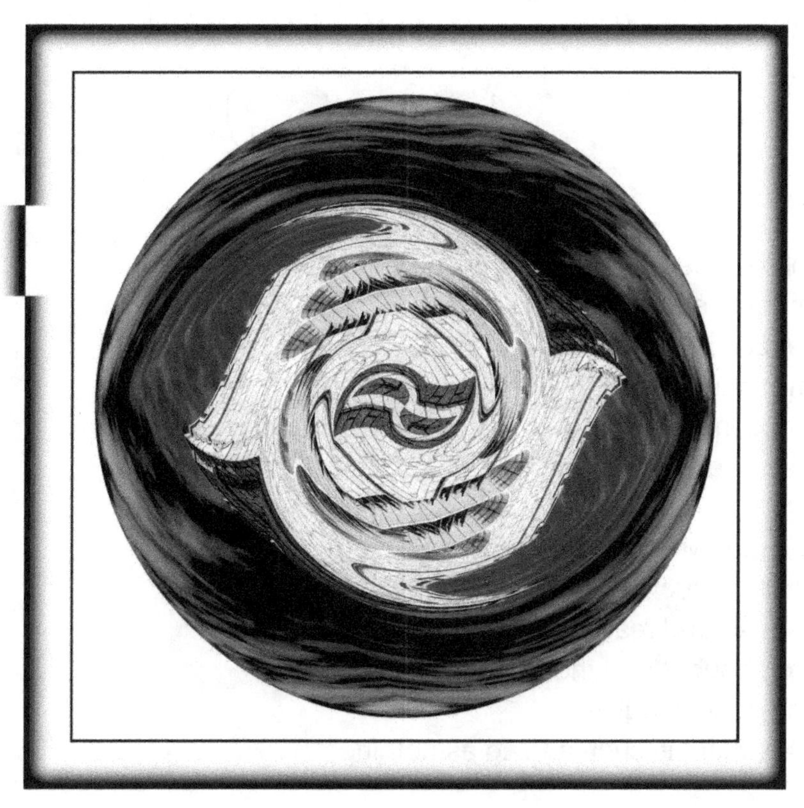

St Columba's R. C. Cathedral

The Old, Wise Philosopher (Things And Nothing)

There once was an old, wise philosopher who asked:
"*Is* there such a thing as a thing…?"
He read and read
And thought and thought
And concluded:
"Yes, there is such a thing as a thing"

The old, wise philosopher then asked:
"*Is* there such a thing as nothing…?"
He read and read
And thought and thought
And concluded:
"Yes, there is such a thing as nothing"

The old, wise philosopher then asked:
"*Could* a thing be nothing?"
He read and read
And thought and thought
And concluded:
"No, a thing could not be nothing"

The old, wise philosopher then asked:
"*Could* nothing be a thing?"
He read and read
And thought and thought
And concluded:
"Yes, nothing could be a thing"

The old, wise philosopher then asked:
"*Would* a thing be nothing?"
He read and read
And thought and thought
And concluded:
"No, a thing would not be nothing"

The old, wise philosopher then asked:
"*Would* nothing be a thing?"
He read and read
And thought and thought
And concluded:
"Yes, nothing would be a thing"

The old, wise philosopher then asked:
"*Should* a thing be nothing?"
He read and read
And thought and thought
And concluded:
"No, a thing should not be nothing"

The old, wise philosopher then asked:
"*Should* nothing be a thing?"
He read and read
And thought and thought
And concluded:
"Yes, nothing should be a thing"

The old, wise philosopher then asked:
"*Can* a thing be nothing?"
He read and read
And thought and thought
And concluded:
"Yes, a thing can be nothing"

The old, wise philosopher then asked:
"*Can* nothing be a thing?"
He read and read
And thought and thought
And concluded:
"Yes, nothing can be a thing"

Why are there things?
Why is there nothing?
What are things?
What is nothing?
Where are things?
Where is nothing?
Who are things?
Who is nothing?
Who is who?
...God is who

If there is such a thing as a thing,
then there is such a thing as truth

If there is such a thing as nothing,
then there is also such a thing as truth

If a thing can be nothing,
then there can be truth

If nothing can be a thing,
then there can also be truth

So, nothing and things can both be truth...

Why is there truth?
What is truth?
Where is truth?
Who is truth?
...God is truth

How can we know God?
How can we know truth?
How can we know things?
How can we know nothing?

If things and nothing exists,
then truth exists

If truth exists,
then God exists,
because God is truth

Without God there is no truth

No God, no truth

No God, no knowledge of things

No God, no knowledge of nothing

No God, no knowledge, and therefore no truth

Denial of God is denial of truth

Denial of God is denial of history

Denial of God is denial of things

Denial of God is denial of nothing

Acceptance of God is acceptance of nothing

Acceptance of God is acceptance of things

Acceptance of God is acceptance of history

Acceptance of God is acceptance of truth

Then the old, wise philosopher concluded:

"God can be found in things
God can be found in nothing
God can be found in history
because God is truth

"No God, no truth"

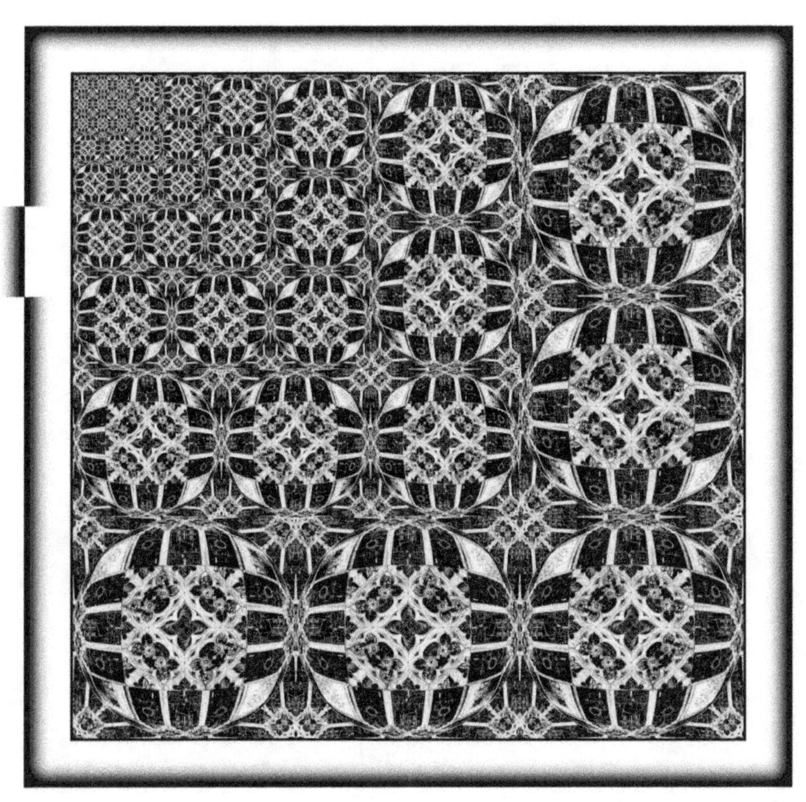

St George's Church, Beckenham

Audiobook on double CD

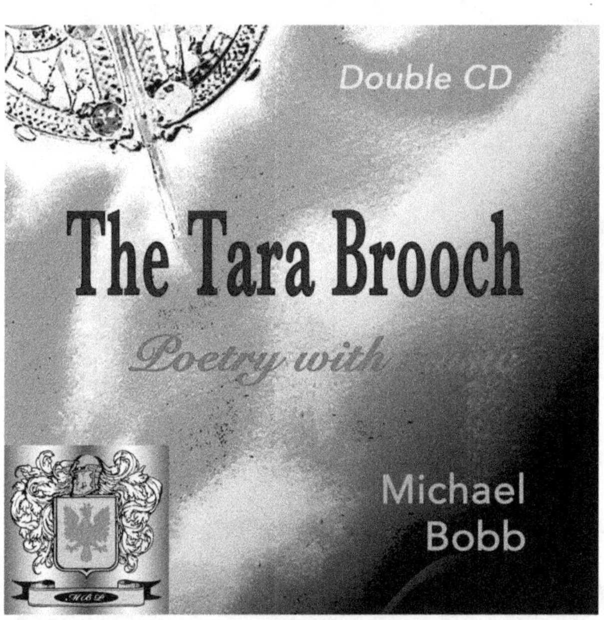

The Tara Brooch

CD 1 *(57 min)*		CD 2 *(71 min)*	
1. The Myth of the Tara Brooch	2:42	1. These Words are by Far Few	3:04
2. Good Morning	1:48	2. The Armour of God	6:02
3. Good Afternoon	2:21	3. The Lion of Judah	4:01
4. Good Night	3:04	4. The Ecstasy of Hildegard	4:13
5. If Only I Could Dream	7:22	5. I Wish I was a Kite	4:33
6. The Maiden's Dream	8:27	6. Leonardo da Vinci 1452 to 1519	2:38
7. Tick-Tock, Tick-Tock	3:53	7. Florestan and Eusebius	3:49
8. It Must Have Taken Hours and Hours	1:45	8. Hermes and Icarus	2:53
9. High Shone the Shining Sun	1:26	9. Mr Spock Finds Cupid's Bow and Arrow	4:20
10. The Heavens are Full of Stars	2:12	10. Blow, You Icy Windy!	3:04
11. Bumble-Bee	1:57	11. Ode to the Quadrature	1:48
12. Feathers (Part 1)	5:29	12. Checkmate! The Queen-Bishop Attack	3:32
13. Feathers (Part 2)	6:03	13. What Did the Little Bird Say?	2:27
14. The Cairns of Ingleborough	4:11	14. I am a Dainty Butterfly	2:09
15. My Everyday Oban	2:10	15. Summer Wind (with Prologue)	10:56
16. She	1:42	16. The Old Wise Philosopher (Things and Nothing)	11:28

All poems have been written and performed by Michael Bobb

Music by: Newman, J. S. Bach, Schubert, Chopin, Arvo Part, Patrick Hawes, Joseph Haydn, Giles Farnaby, F. T., Robin Holloway, Michael Bobb, W. A. Mozart, Robert Schumann, Vivaldi, D. Scarlatti, Richard Farnaby, Tchaikovsky

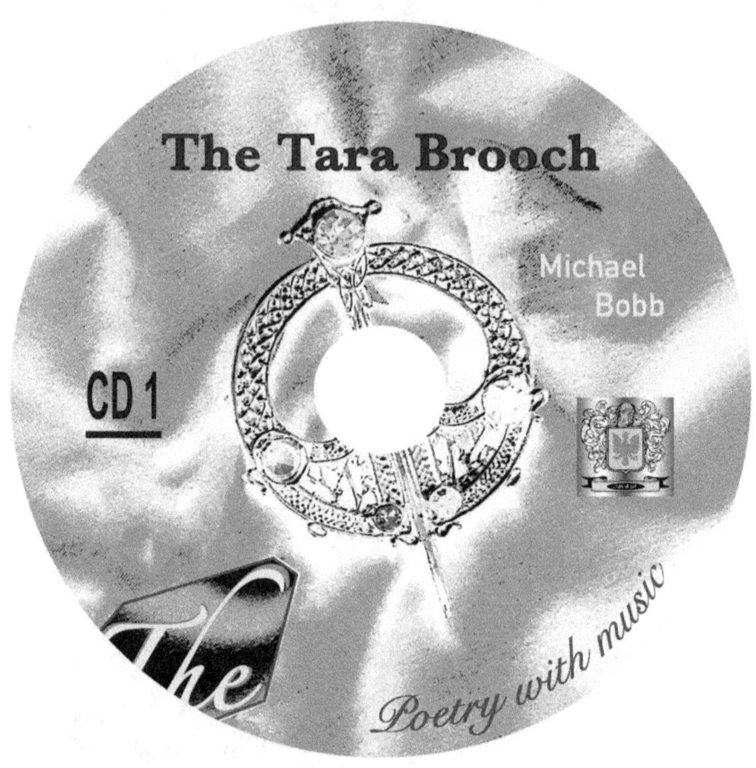

The Tara Brooch
Michael Bobb
CD 1
The
Poetry with music

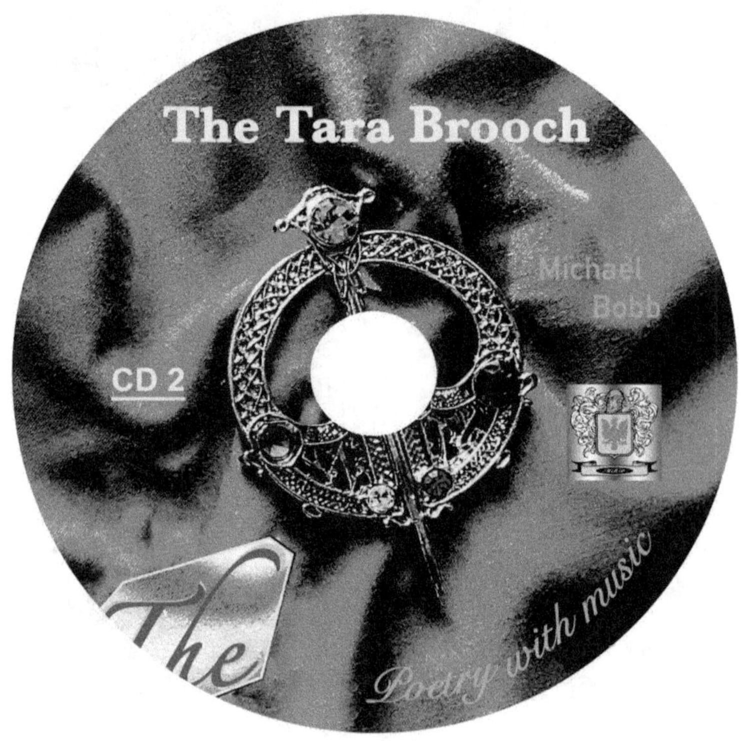

The Tara Brooch
Michael Bobb
CD 2
The
Poetry with music

Audiobook on YouTube

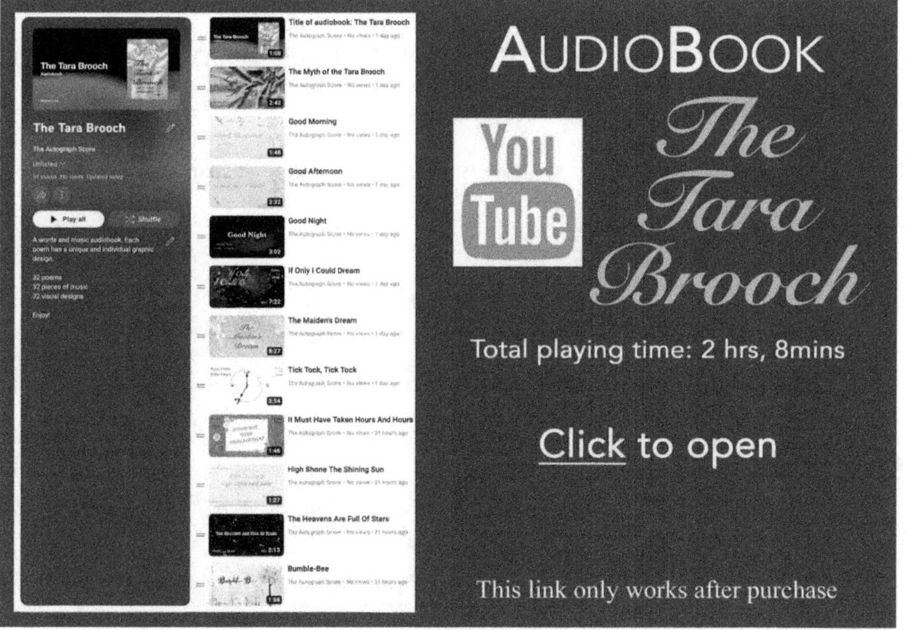

Available from

The Autograph Score

www.theautographscore.co.uk

Music in audiobook

1. The Myth Of The Tara Brooch   *(Newman — A Pavyon from Mulliner's Book)*

2. Good Morning   *(J. S. Bach — Sheep May Safely Graze from Cantata 208)*

3. Good Afternoon   *(Franz Schubert — Serenade)*

4. Good Night   *(Frédéric Chopin — Nocturne in Eb major, Op. 9, No. 2)*

5. If Only I Could Dream   *(Arvo Pärt — Spiegel Im Spiegel)*

6. The Maiden's Dream   *(Patrick Hawes — Quanta Qualia)*

7. Tick-Tock, Tick-Tock   *(Joseph Haydn — Clock Symphony, No. 101)*

8. It Must Have Taken Hours And Hours   *(Giles Farnaby — Alman)*

9. High Shone The Shining Sun   *(F. T. — La Bounette from Mulliner's Book)*

10. The Heaven's Are Full Of Stars   *(J. S. Bach — Partita No. 1, Giga)*

11. Bumble-Bee   *(Robin Holloway — Scherzino from Partitina on J. S. Bach's 'Goldberg')*

12. Feathers (Part 1) *(Patrick Hawes — Stargazer)*

13. Feathers (Part 2) *(Patrick Hawes — Stargazer)*

14. The Cairns Of Ingleborough *(Michael Bobb — Antonia)*

15. My Everyday Oban *(Highland Cathedral)*

16. She *(W. A. Mozart — Andante Grazioso and Variation No. 1 from Sonata No. 11)*

17. These Words Are By Far Few *(Robert Schumann — Widmung)*

18. The Armour Of GOD *(Vivaldi — Cum Sancto Spiritu from Gloria RV 589)*

19. The Lion Of Judah *(Michael Bobb — Greensleeves Variation No. 3, "The Agitator Alla Toccata")*

20. The Ecstasy Of Hildegard *(J. S. Bach — Lord, Though A-while In Tears Of Sorrow from St. Matthew Passion)*

21. I Wish I Was A Kite *(D. Scarlatti — Sonata in G, Kp. 259)*

22. Leonardo da Vinci 1452-1519 *(Richard Farnaby — Fain would I wed)*

23. Florestan And Eusebius *(Frédéric Chopin — Ballade No. 1)*

24. Hermes And Icarus *(Tchaikovsky — Dance of the Reed Flutes from The Nutcracker)*

25. Mr Spock Finds Cupid's Bow And Arrow *(Franz Schubert — Scherzo No. 1 from D593)*

26. Blow, You Icy Windy! *(Rimsky-Korsakov — The Flight of the Bumble-Bee)*

27. Checkmate! The Queen-Bishop Attack *(Gustav Holst — Mars from 'The Planets')*

28. Ode To The Quadrature *(J. S. Bach — Fugue No. 1 in C Major from W-T C Bk 1)*

29. What Did The Little Bird Say...? *(Franz Schubert — Scherzo from Piano Sonata in E, D459)*

30. I am A Dainty Butterfly *(Gabriel Fauré — Berceuse from Dolly Suite)*

31. Summer Wind (with Prologue) *(Khachaturian — Adagio of Spartacus and Phrygia from Spartacus)*

32. The Old, Wise Philosopher (Things And Nothing) *(J. S. Bach — The Art of the Fugue, Contrapunctus I)*

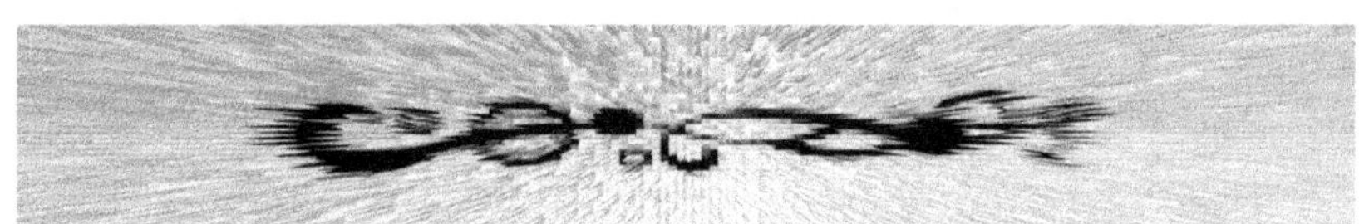

www.ingramcontent.com/pod-product-compliance
Lightning Source LLC
Chambersburg PA
CBHW071452030726
47593CB00003B/972